Wild Flowers of the Northeastern States

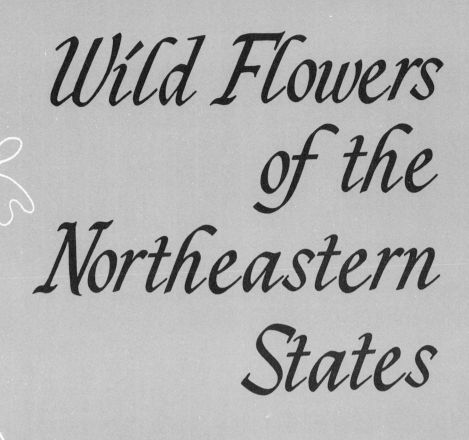

Wild Flowers
of the
Northeastern
States

THE NEW YORK BOTANICAL GARDEN

Text and Slides by FREDERICK W. CASE, JR.

McGraw-Hill Book Company
New York   St. Louis   San Francisco   Auckland
Bogotá   Düsseldorf   Johannesburg   London
Madrid   Mexico   Montreal   New Delhi
Panama   São Paulo   Singapore
Sydney   Tokyo   Toronto

Library of Congress Cataloging in Publication Data

New York (City). Botanical Garden.
  Wild flowers of the Northeastern States.

  Text and color slides by F. W. Case, Jr.
  1. Wild flowers—Northeastern States. 2. Wild
flowers—Pictorial works.
I. Case, Frederick W. II. Title.
QK117.N48 1978   582'.13'0974   77-17439
ISBN 0-07-046371-9

1234567890 DAAH 7654321098

The editors for this book were Robert A. Rosenbaum and Joan Zseleczky,
the designer was Naomi Auerbach, and the production supervisor
was Teresa F. Leaden. It was set in Palatino
by University Graphics, Inc.

Printed by Davis Printing Corporation and bound by
A. Horowitz & Son Bookbinders.

Contents

Preface

I do not intend these slides or this text to serve as an identification manual. Many fine field guides to flowers of the Northeast exist today. My purpose in writing this book is to provide, for the uninitiated laypersons or those casually interested in wild flowers and their habitats, attractive color slides and enough information about plants to challenge the viewer-reader to go from these essays and slides to a deeper study and appreciation of wild plants and their environments.

Wild flowers, like wild animals, display fascinating structural and behavioral adaptations for survival. And plants are every bit as sensitive to environmental conditions as are animals. They grow where they do because the conditions at that spot meet their needs. Finding them in the wild, understanding the complexities of their ecology, and cultivating them in the garden is exciting and rewarding. It is but a short step to go from appreciation and personal enjoyment of these plants to the realization of how desperate is the need for their conservation. I firmly believe that an informed public is the strongest weapon we have for conservation in a democracy. Conservation laws passed can also be rescinded. But if the public believes in the value of living things, understands the complexities of their life cycles, and knows and enjoys the plants and animals that have evolved in the nature about us, then it will demand protection for this heritage and will support the laws intended to conserve threatened and endangered species.

Through this book I hope to obtain converts to the fascinating study of native plants and to convince them of the worth of wild-flower conservation.

The selection of the particular species and habitats discussed in the book is mine. Guided by the publisher's stipulation that they be plants and habitats occurring in the New York State region, I have selected them further to be species typical of those habitats and to strike a balance between common and rare species. I have also tried to choose plants of special interest. The limitation to forty slides necessarily restricts this coverage.

Preceding each group of plant essays is a very brief discussion of the general conditions in which the species grow. I present the species in approximate phenological order, but this order does vary somewhat from one area to another.

I have used the common names of the plants which are now in use or have been generally used in the Northeastern states for generations. I have not used some of the standardized plant names deliberately improvised or devised by some authors. Such names often do not reflect common usage or the rich folklore history of the plants involved.

The Latin names are those adopted by Fernald in *Gray's New Manual of Botany,* eighth edition.

I am grateful to the staff members of the New York Botanical Garden, to the editors, and to my wife for their advice and help in preparing the manuscript.

Frederick W. Case, Jr.

Wild Flowers of the Northeastern States

THE EASTERN DECIDUOUS FOREST

The climate of the Eastern United States east of the 100th meridian generally favors the development of a deciduous forest community rich in species. Such a large area spans regions of great differences in soils, rainfall, and summer and winter temperatures. The differences are reflected in the various groups of species of trees which dominate the forest locally. Herbaceous plants and wild flowers, too, differ locally in occurrence and abundance. Some species grow wholly within certain districts, while others range beyond the cover of specific trees or the confines of exact soil types. The latter seem adapted to the general conditions common throughout the deciduous forest and grow wherever it occurs.

Within this forest, thick layers of decaying leaves frequently cover the soil. In summer the canopy of green leaves allows little light to reach the herbs on the forest floor.

Most species of wild flowers of this forest expanse bloom in early spring. They have adapted to take advantage of the brief early period of sunlight and available moisture which follows the last spring frosts and precedes the appearance of the leafy canopy in May.

The wild flowers of the deciduous forest produced their flower and leaf buds for this spring last year. These buds lay dormant over the winter on buried roots or rhizomes. With springtime warming, the preformed tissues absorb water, expand, and become flowers almost at once. Then, following pollination, and as the leaves expand, the plants manufacture food, develop seeds, and prepare for next season by again producing rudimentary leaf and flower buds.

Soils in the deciduous forest, at least in upland places, tend to be reasonably well drained and subacid to neutral in reaction, and they resemble closely those regarded as good gardening soils. Consequently, the commoner plants of this forest can often be cultivated in shaded areas in ordinary gardens.

Wild Flowers of the Eastern Deciduous Forest

1. Yellow Adder's-Tongue (*Erythronium americanum*)
2. Bloodroot (*Sanguinaria canadensis*)
3. Spring Beauty (*Claytonia virginica*)
4. Dutchman's-Breeches (*Dicentra cucullaria*)
5. Squirrel Corn (*Dicentra canadensis*)
6. Red Trillium (*Trillium erectum*)
7. White Trillium (*Trillium grandiflorum*)
8. Wild Blue Phlox (*Phlox divaricata*)
9. Large-flowered Bellwort (*Uvularia grandiflora*)
10. Wild Ginger (*Asarum canadense*)
11. Jack-in-the-Pulpit (*Arisaema triphyllum*)
12. Wild Geranium (*Geranium maculatum*)
13. Patridgeberry (*Mitchella repens*)
14. Indian Pipe (*Monotropa uniflora*)

SLIDE 1 **Yellow Adder's-Tongue, Dogtooth Violet, Trout Lily**

Erythronium americanum Ker.

Almost every rural schoolboy knows the mottled leaves of this plant. It grows in deciduous forests throughout the East, its leaves forming great patches on the forest floor. Many colonies, however, produce few blossoms in a given season. There are a number of reasons for this. Shade, soil fertility, crowding, and competition from other species all affect blooming. But two factors predominate. The first is a time factor: the plants require from five to eight years to mature. Many nonflowering plants are immature. A second factor is the pattern of growth. Seedlings germinate near the surface of the ground. Mature, flowering-sized bulbs occur at a depth of about 7 inches. As the seedling develops, a shoot grows from this season's bulb and penetrates deeper into the ground to produce next season's bulb. Thus the bulb is projected deeper and deeper into the ground as the plant matures. Under some habitat conditions, plants actually penetrate to such depths that they must convert so much stored food to send the leaf to the surface that the plant becomes too weak to bloom. One noted wild-flower grower has solved the problem of getting the plants to bloom in his garden. When planting a clump of adder's-tongue bulbs, he digs a deep hole and places a flat rock below the bulbs at about the 7-inch depth. The bulbs, unable to grow deeper, expend their energy in producing blooms.

The six floral segments, consisting of three sepals and three petals (or six tepals), are colored and textured alike and respond to changes in light intensity. At night and during dark days, these tepals remain closed and budlike. In bright sunlight the flower segments quickly reflex and the blossom becomes bell-like. The backs of the flower segments are relatively dull-colored, but the inner surfaces are a rich yellow, sometimes with flecks of maroon near the base, and are very showy for the size of the plant. The conspicuous stamens can be maroon, brown, or yellow. Developing seedpods become so heavy that the delicate flowering stem cannot hold them erect, so they bend to the ground to mature and disperse their seeds there.

The colorful common names of this species derive from characteristics of flower, leaf, or bulb. "Adder's-tongue" alludes to the conspicuous stigmas extending from the somewhat gaping petals and sepals rather like a serpent's forked tongue. The name "dogtooth violet" originates with the shape of the pointed, solid bulb, which resembles the cuspid or canine tooth of a dog. A fancied similarity between the light and dark mottling of the leaves and the markings on the back of trout accounts for the name "trout lily."

The 1- to 2-dm-tall flower scapes appear very early in the season, mostly from late March to mid-April. Each bloom lasts five to twelve days. Adapted to produce food quickly before the expanding tree leaves shut out the light, the plant's leaves wither and disappear before the end of May.

Yellow adder's-tongue ranges across most of the Eastern deciduous forest, from Canada south to Alabama and Georgia, and westward to the prairie provinces. It is still a common and beautiful flower.

SLIDE 2 **Bloodroot**

Sanguinaria canadensis L.

The flowering scapes and leaves of bloodroot arise from a perennial, fleshy underground rhizome. The leaves at first simply clasp the stem below the flower but later enlarge and extend beyond the ripened capsule. The leaves are palmately 3- to 9-lobed, cleft at the apex, prominently veined, especially below, and covered with a conspicuous, whitish, dustlike bloom. Leaf blade and petiole together measure 1 to 3.5 dm tall, expanding rapidly after blooming.

Flowering scapes are one-flowered and of variable height depending upon the age of the plant, the extent of development time which has elapsed in a given season, plant vigor, and whether the bloom is on the main rhizome or on a branch. Commonly, scapes reach a height of 10 to 15 cm.

Flowers open only in bright light. Petals are white or rarely pinkish or bluish, especially on their backs; they are 2 to 2½ cm long, narrow, and very quickly falling. It is not uncommon, if the day is windy, for petals to remain on the plant only a few hours. The usual eight to twelve petals form a squarish flower of beautiful symmetry and surface texture, set off with the orange-yellow stamens. A double form in which all stamens have become petals is one of the most prized garden wild flowers today.

Bloodroot forms large patches in woodlands and is hardy enough to persist in fencerows and pastures for years after the trees have been removed. It also seeds about readily in cultivation.

Besides its delicate beauty, the plant possesses another interesting feature. The juice of the rhizome is a bright red or rust color. When the rhizome is cut or broken, it oozes drops of "blood." When this juice is smeared upon the skin, the color is orange red. Indians used the plant as a source of war paint and as a coloring for decorating garments and pottery, even though the dye is water-soluble.

Bloodroot ranges from Nova Scotia to Manitoba and southward to Alabama and Florida. It blooms very early in the growing season, in March, April, and May.

SLIDE 3 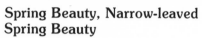 **Spring Beauty, Narrow-leaved Spring Beauty**
Claytonia virginica L.

Spring Beauty develops in earliest spring from a very deeply buried fleshy tuber. Often the tuber is so deep that in attempting to dig it up one misses it entirely. Yet the Indians are said to have used it as food. From each stem above the tuber springs a pair of opposite, fleshy, linear grasslike leaves, and above these a raceme of small but delicately showy flowers. A single tuber may bear up to forty flowering stems.

The blossoms, typically less than an inch in diameter, have a very delicate sparkling sheen, and are white or pink, almost always with much deeper coloring in the veins. The two persistent and clasping sepals remain quite conspicuous after the petals have fallen.

Although much smaller, the blossoms of spring beauty closely resemble those of its larger Western relatives, the bitterroots or lewisias.

Narrow-leaved spring beauty occurs over much of Eastern North America from Quebec and Minnesota southward to Georgia and Alabama. It prefers to grow in low, moist flatwoods, often in a heavy, clayey soil. In New York it is frequent near the coast but is replaced by a similar but broader-leaved species, *Claytonia caroliniana* Michx., the broad-leaved spring beauty, in the interior and in upland habitats.

The spring beauties are subject to a rustlike infection. In many woodlots, most of the flower racemes develop orangish granular pustules which badly damage the developing seedpods, often causing the entire raceme to yellow and shrivel. The disease seems not to injure the plants permanently, for they appear and bloom again in subsequent seasons.

Spring beauty is easy to grow in any wild garden and requires only that the soil be well drained, not soggy.

SLIDE 4 🌺 Dutchman's-Breeches
Dicentra cucullaria (L.) Bernh.

That Dutchman's-breeches is a close relative of the bleeding heart group can be instantly recognized, for in these plants the spurs of the outer pair of four petals form the characteristically heart-shaped profile. And too, the much-divided, bluish-green leaves, although smaller and more delicate, closely resemble those of the garden bleeding heart. The row of nodding flowers borne on a somewhat arching spike is among the most familiar of spring flowers.

The foliage of this species is among the first to appear in rich but well-drained deciduous woodlands, and may be well developed even when heavy frost still occurs nightly. In early- to mid-April at the latitude of New York or New England, the flower spikes are thrust up above the foliage. Development is rapid on warm days, and the Dutchman's-breeches in snowy white or pale pink with yellow tips quickly appear. The flowers are eagerly visited by honeybees and bumblebees. Often, in their eagerness to obtain the nectar and pollen, the bees bite holes in the spurs of the flower to get at the food, rather than pry apart the complexly closed petals to enter by the normal route.

The leaves and flowers spring from a closely clustered bulb, the individual segments of which look like grains of rice. One of the first plants to appear in the spring, it is also one of the first to disappear in May after leaves of trees shade it. Its photosynthetic process must be enormously efficient to enable the plant to produce leaves, flowers, and seeds, make new buds for the next season, and store sufficient food, all in so few days of early spring.

SLIDE 5 🌺 Squirrel Corn, Turkey Corn
Dicentra canadensis (Goldie) Walp.

Another close relative of the bleeding heart, and an even closer relative of the Dutchman's-breeches, the squirrel corn is familiar to those who roam the springtime woods. Squirrel corn often grows near or intermingled with Dutchman's-breeches. In some districts, however, the two species only rarely occur in the same woods. In the Great Lakes region, at least, squirrel corn occurs most abundantly in sandy moraine soils, situations which get drier in summer than the soils chosen by Dutchman's-breeches.

Squirrel corn's habit above ground is quite similar to that of Dutchman's-breeches—a tuft of finely or much-divided blue-green leaves and a somewhat arching spike of six to ten flowers, nodding, bleeding-heart-like in configuration or form and white to pinkish in color. In the squirrel corn, however, the flower spurs of the outer two petals are shorter, are rounded instead of more or less pointed, and do not diverge. Whereas the blooms of Dutchman's-breeches viewed upside down, look distinctly like a pair of Dutch pantaloons, those of squirrel corn are more heart-shaped. In parts of New England, children refer to the two species as "boys" (*D. cucullaria*), and "girls" (*D. canadensis*). Indeed, if the bloom of squirrel corn is viewed upside down, the flower profile does resemble the shape of a girl in a long skirt.

The underground parts of the two species differ, as do the blooms. Instead of the closely clustered, rice-grain-like bulb, the squirrel corn has scattered, bright-yellow tubers about the size of corn grains. The derivation of the common name of the plant is obvious.

Both species of *Dicentra* occur throughout New England and from the Maritime Provinces of Canada to Minnesota and South Dakota southward, but squirrel corn has a more restricted range, reaching south only to North Carolina and Missouri, while Dutchman's-breeches ranges south to Georgia and Alabama. Both species are easily cultivated but do not bloom freely until well established again after being moved.

The Trilliums Plants of the genus *Trillium* are among the best known and best loved of native American wild flowers. This widespread genus is divided into two sections: plants which bear their flowers above the leaves on a short stalk or peduncle, and those which develop the flowers directly upon the leaves (that is, with sessile flowers). Plants of this latter group have interesting and often showy leaves heavily mottled in patterns of dark and light green and maroon. In the Northeast and New England, the sessile-flowered trilliums do not occur as natives, but several species of the pedunculate (stalk-flowered) trilliums do.

As their name implies, all trilliums bear three leaves. In the species frequent in New York and the Northeast, the leaves are usually broadly rhombic. Those of the white trillium usually have a dark red-purple pigment underlying the green; those of the red trillium do not. In normal flowers, the sepals, petals, and stigmas occur in threes, along with six stamens, usually with large, conspicuous anthers (pollen sacs).

Since trilliums bear their flowers either directly upon the leaves or on a short, 1- to 2-inch peduncle, the plants should be admired where they grow and their blossoms should not be picked; blossom-picking inevitably includes the leaves and thus deprives the underground stem and roots of their food-making organs and seriously weakens the plants. None of the trilliums is capable of initiating a second set of leaves or flowers in the same growing season if the original stem is injured or destroyed. A period of rest and low temperatures is required to break dormancy in buds. The relatively great lengths of time necessary for a damaged plant to "coast" on stored food limits the plant's ability to recover from the damage that results when a stem has been broken.

 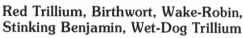

SLIDE 6

Red Trillium, Birthwort, Wake-Robin, Stinking Benjamin, Wet-Dog Trillium
Trillium erectum L.

This charming trillium blooms early in the Northeastern United States and Canada. Although less conspicuous than its large, white-flowered relative, it is still showy and uncommonly interesting. Its Latin name suggests strictly erect flowering stalks, but the typical plant's bloom tends to lean at an angle which renders it less showy than if it really were borne erect. In typical plants the petals are somewhat elongated and of a dark red-maroon color when fresh. They soon fade, however, to a more dull purple maroon. The dark flower color attracts certain flies and beetles which are the pollinators for this species. Like so many plants with dark red, brown, or lurid maroon and green flowers, the red trillium produces a fetid odor to aid in attracting its carrion-seeking pollinators. The distinctly wet-dog-like odor gives the plant its most quaint common names. Fortunately, the smell is perceptible only at very close range.

The flowers last up to three or more weeks. If pollinated, the blossom produces a dark, purple-black, six-angled berry which in vigorous plants attains the size of a cherry when mature. The berry, with a definitely fruitlike fragrance, contains a number of hard-coated seeds, each with a tiny appendage (aril) of oil-filled tissue. As with all trilliums, the seeds are especially attractive to ants, which often remove the seeds from the berry even before it ripens fully. The ants bury the seeds in their nests and eat the oily aril, leaving the seed itself alone. After a long and complicated temperature-governed ripening process, sometimes taking over two years, the seeds germinate in the ant storehouses. It is easy to find seedlings which have obviously germinated in ant seed caches, growing so crowded together that many can never survive. Maturation of the plants requires up to six or seven years.

The wake-robin enjoys a particularly wide range, extending from Quebec southward to the Smoky Mountains of Tennessee, and westward, locally in upland regions on the Cumberland Plateau northward through parts of Ohio and the lower peninsula of Michigan. Although wake-robin has been reported from farther west in the Midland states, such reports usually refer to color forms of *T. flexipes* Raf. (*T. gleasonii*).

Red trillium has only a few really critical growth requirements: cool soil, moderate acidity, and somewhat more mositure than in the habitats preferred by its relative, the white trillium. While the red trillium is a legally protected plant in some states, it is not rare where suitable habitat occurs within its range. It is easily grown in woodland gardens, rhododendron beds, or similar sites, but it should not be collected indiscriminately or in violation of regional conservation laws.

Almost no other native plant has so many color forms or mutations. Apparently, many genes together govern the color of a petal. If all function normally, the color of the fresh flower is a dark maroon purple. If some of the genes are altered through mutation, petals may be light purple, pinkish, yellow, cream, greenish, or white. Certain of the color factors seem to control only a portion of the petal. Some of the mutations, therefore, produce petals with basal blotches which differ in color from that of the petal tips. Besides these mutations, hybrids between *T. erectum* and *T. flexipes* are formed wherever the ranges and habitats occur near each other. The hybrids vary even more than the mutants and introduce interesting blotching to the outside of the petals. In several Midwest localities, both species, their mutations, and innumerable hybrids and backcrosses occur. The result is a mosaic of beautiful color forms.

Look for the wake-robin in mature deciduous forests where the soil is rich but somewhat acid. It is often found on slopes of ravines under hemlocks, or on small valley flats near streams. In the Eastern mountains it ascends to considerable elevations and often occurs among rhododendron thickets. It may mingle with the white trillium in some districts and yet in other districts remain apart from the white trillium even when growing in the same woods.

In mature deciduous forests undisturbed by pasturing or recreational vehicles, it is more than capable of holding its own. But disturbances to its shade cover or to its water supply, as by lumbering, which allows excessive soil heating, rapidly decimate its populations.

SLIDE 7 ❀ **White Trillium, Common Trillium**
Trillium grandiflorum (Michx.) Salisb.

The white trillium occurs abundantly over much of its range and is probably the best-known flower of the spring woodlands. Its three gleaming-white petals and bright-yellow stamens make it by far the showiest of the trilliums. The white petals turn rose pink with age; if the season is quite cool, the rose color may be very dark. Forms also occur in which the flowers open pale pink. Double-flowered forms occur, either the "hose-in-hose" type (three petals set within another set of three, a flower within a flower) or full doubles in which all floral organs have converted to petals so that the bloom resembles a peony or a camellia.

In some districts flowers appear with green stripes in the petals, or with green and white blotching. Sometimes the leaves on these strange forms may be entirely wanting or greatly modified. This condition, often referred to as a "sport," is actually the result of a mycoplasmalike disease caused by an ultramicroscopic organism living in the plant's cells. The organism seems to have an almost genelike ability to alter the plant's development.

The white trillium grows in a variety of woods and brushy thickets but clearly prefers moderately mature hardwoods dominated by beech, maple, and hemlock. In suitable habitats with rich, sandy-humusy soils, massive colonies of hundreds of thousands of plants may develop over hundreds of acres.

This species ranges from Quebec and Maine westward to eastern Minnesota and southward in the uplands to Georgia. Common plant companions of this trillium include the trout lilies, hepaticas, Dutchman's-breeches, and spurred voilets.

There are several white-flowered trilliums in the Northeast, but no other species bears such large, *upright* blooms. The petals are also of a delicate, texture, rather than thick or leathery, with the major veins slightly depressed on the petal's upper surface.

This plant is highly prized in Europe as one of America's most glorious gifts to the world's gardens. It is seldom seen in regular garden borders in this country but is ever present in special wild-flower gardens. Although protected in some states, it is not seriously endangered except locally where urbanization threatens its habitats. Very mild disturbances such as selective lumbering or gentle pasturing actually improve the habitat and may cause the colonies to increase.

SLIDE 8 ✿ **Wild Blue Phlox**

Phlox divaricata L.

Most people know the phloxes from the large-flowered garden varieties, but few realize that the phloxes are almost entirely of American origin (one Alaskan species occurs also in Siberia). Authorities differ in their interpretation of species limits, but the number of species and subspecies of *Phlox* is large. The greatest numbers occur in the Western and Southeastern states, often in desert or alpine situations. A number of interesting and very beautiful species of intermediate or large size occur in the East. Of these, the one most likely to be encountered in the rich Eastern deciduous forests is *Phlox divaricata*, the wild blue phlox.

The blooms, in a spreading flat cluster called a "cyme," are tubular, with large, notched petal lobes. The color ranges from good clear blues through lavender tones to almost dingy grey-lavenders. Occasionally albino forms occur. Regardless of color type, the blooms produce a delicious spicy fragrance. Blooming stems range from 1.5 to 5 dm in height. The plant spreads loosely from central tufts of opposite leaves (but those of the flowering stems may alternate).

In suitable woods, usually in low, heavy soils, often near streams, great drifts of this phlox grow. The plant occurs from Vermont and Quebec westward to Michigan and Illinois and southward to South Carolina and Alabama. In New York State, it is more common west of the coastal regions.

Because it is a very fine subject for the wild garden or perennial border, this phlox is widely grown, and several fine horticultural forms have appeared. Planted in any reasonably rich, moist soil, the phlox thrives. It tolerates full sun or light shade. In wild gardens, it appears particularly at home with Christmas ferns, hepaticas, adder's-tongue lilies, and trilliums. It is fully compatible with plants of the perennial border as well. It is neither rare nor particularly endangered. If it is grown from collected plants, the gardener ought to take pains to collect good colors and fine flower forms.

The species has escaped from cultivation into surrounding woodlands in districts where it formerly did not grow natively.

SLIDE 9 ✿ **Large-flowered Bellwort, Wild Oats**

Uvularia grandiflora Smith

Large-flowered Bellwort occurs typically in rich, upland deciduous forests, usually in neutral soil. It is a characteristic plant of mature woods, where it grows in company with Canada violet, trilliums, Dutchman's-breeches, sharp-lobed hepaticas, and Christmas ferns.

Bellwort appears early, and flowers may develop before total expansion of the stem occurs. The plant may produce single stems or form scattered clumps. The seasonal stems arise from a perennial underground rhizome and reach a height of 7 dm or more. The leaves, at least the lower ones, are perfoliate, that is, the stem appears to pass right through the leaf base. Actually, in the developmental history of the species, the lobes surrounded the stem and fused beyond it. In this species the undersurface of the leaves is finely pubescent, while in the similar species, *U. perfoliata* L., it is smooth. Solitary, drooping flowers appear at the ends of short branches. Blossoms range from lemon yellow to light orange yellow; the sepals and petals are alike in color and texture. Regularly the outer portion of the petal is somewhat twisted, giving the entire flower a slightly spiraled look. Because of the drooping nature of the bloom, it nearly always appears to be not quite fully opened.

An easy plant to cultivate, the species is also quite common in most districts within its range.

SLIDE 10 ✿ **Wild Ginger, Indian Ginger**

Asarum canadense L.

The soft green and velvety, kidney-shaped, paired leaves of wild ginger form patches on the forest floor of rich low and moist woodland from New Brunswick to Manitoba southward to North Carolina, Missouri, and Kansas. The leaves, 7 to 18 cm broad, arise at intervals from a branching rhizome creeping on the soil surface. The entire plant is densely fine pubescent. At the time of blooming, in April and May, the leaves only partly expand. The flower, borne on a short, slender peduncle from between the petiole bases, usually is buried under old leaves and forest litter on the ground. The three-cornered bloom, 2 to 3 cm long and broad, consists of three sepals fused to the large and fleshy ovary. Only the lobes of the sepals remain free and spreading reflexed, and drawn out into long tapered tips. Flower color is brownish purple, maroon, or greenish. The odor is faintly fetid. Both the odor and placement of the blossom are adaptations of the plant for pollination, for the plant is pollinated by crawling beetles, flies, and carrion-seeking insects which are attracted by the color and odor of the bloom. Within this species considerable variation in flower size, coloring, and sepal tip shape exists.

The name "wild ginger" derives from the pungent-aromatic odor of the bruised rhizome, but it is not the true ginger of commerce.

A common plant and easily cultivated, it forms a most useful ground cover in shaded areas and ought to be more widely grown.

In the Southeastern United States several related species grow; these are placed by some botanists into another genus, *Hexastylis.* In this group, the leaves are evergreen, smooth, and often leathery, and marked with obscure-to-prominent light-green or silvery patterns. Flowers may be more or less showy than in wild ginger. Like wild ginger, these plants have garden value.

SLIDE 11  ## Jack-in-the-Pulpit, Indian Turnip
Arisaema triphyllum (L.) Schott

Some plants excite human imagination more than others. Few native American plants have succeeded in attaining the popularity of the jack-in-the-pulpit. Its bulblike corm, sheathed stalk, the one or two sets of leaves divided into three leaflets each, and above all the quaint, striped or mottled spathe arising between the leaves with its little clublike spadix—the "preacher in his pulpit"—make this one of the best known and loved of our native plants.

A member of the worldwide arum family, jack-in-the-pulpit shares many features with its relatives. Members of this family share not only structural similarities, but physiological ones as well. Most manufacture and store an abundance of starch which humans around the world utilize for food. They produce not only starch but also crystals of an irritating acid. Members of the family, which includes philodendron, dieffenbachia, and calla lilies, cannot be eaten raw. The edible tissues must be boiled for a long period, usually with changes of cooking water, to destroy the crystals. Otherwise, the experience is painful, for the crystals dislodge from the plant tissues and embed in those of the eater. Burning, swelling, and much pain result and the condition can be dangerous. It was once a favorite but unkind trick of country children to dupe their city cousins into tasting the Indian turnip.

Jack-in-the-pulpit grows in a wide variety of moist woodlands. Several forms or races occur, some very tall, with immense green spathes. Others, often associated with swampier habitats, are smaller, with striped spathes of dark maroon-black color alternating with pale greenish white. The various forms are genetic, for when grown side by side they retain their distinctive characteristics. The spathe, really a modified leaf rather than a petal, sheathes the spadix, which bears the tiny, inconspicuous true flowers. A cluster of brilliant scarlet berries develops by autumn. As the season progresses the leaves and the plant stalk slowly deteriorate, and the plant collapses under the weight of the berry cluster.

The species occurs in rich deciduous woods, along streams, in upland swamps, cedar swamps, thickets, and floodplain woods across Eastern America. Some botanists consider that there is but one species, while others believe that several subtle species or varieties exist. When present in a district, the plants of a given variety are usually not rare.

SLIDE 12 ❀ ## Wild Geranium, Spotted Geranium
Geranium maculatum L.

Wild geranium, a very familiar woodland species over much of the deciduous forest zone of the Eastern states and Canada, ranges southward to Georgia and westward to Kansas. Its rather large, rosy purple blossoms light up forest and roadside in May.

The plant is distincly showy, with several stems 2 to 5 dm tall bearing loose clusters of blooms. The large, attractive leaves, circular and deeply toothed or five-lobed, persist for the entire season. The five distinct petals are about 1 to 2 cm long, pale to deep rosy purple, with darker veins. White and pale pink forms occur occasionally.

An unusual feature of the plant is the persistent capsule tipped with the compound style. Upon ripening, the bases of the capsule separate and curl upward, while the tips remain attached to the style. The seeds are released and the remains of the carpels form a recurved hornlike structure, giving the capsule a strange, harpoonlike appearance.

Wild geranium is a hardy, garden-worthy plant that is easily cultivated. Because it is nearly everywhere common, it can be collected judiciously. Perhaps the best policy is to divide a large clump, removing part but leaving part in the wild.

SLIDE 13 ❀ ## Partridgeberry, Squaw Berry, Two-eyed Berry, Twinberry
Mitchella repens L.

Partridgeberry must surely be one of the best known of the trailing, herbaceous ground covers. Its tiny, round-ovate leaves, often with a light green or whitish line or markings, and its scarlet berries adorn not only the woodland floor, but countless dish gardens, terraria, brandy snifters, and antique bottles. Few other plants seem so perfectly built to scale and are so enduring in these popular planters.

Twinberry has a very wide range, from Nova Scotia to western Ontario, and southward to the Ozark Mountains, Texas, and Florida. It tolerates a wide variety of habitats and may be found in old, sandy, moist pastures, as well as in oak, pine, hemlock, birch, and beech-maple forests. It is in the rich, mature deciduous forests, however, that the largest and most vigorous patches occur.

Not only is the matted viny plant evergreen and attractive for its glossy, white-marked leaves, but it is also most attractive in flower or fruit. The fragrant white flowers are borne in pairs. The funnelform bloom is about 12 mm long, with four recurved, lobed tips which are covered with hairs on their inner surfaces. Two types of blossoms may occur: one in which the male organs, the stamens, extend from the corolla (are exserted) while the stigma and style remain hidden within the floral tube, and one in which the female organs, the style and stigma, are exserted, in which case the stamens remain within the tube. In either type of flower, the ovaries of the paired blooms are united at their bases. When fruit develops, it is double; the basal portion shows calyx scars from two blooms. In spite of the name of the plant, the fruit is technically not a berry but a drupe, a fleshy, moist, outer-covering layer over a hard pitlike coating surrounding the true seed. The scarlet fruits may persist on the plant for over a year.

The juices of the leaves are bitterly astringent. Indians are said to have used the plant as a remedy for stomach disorders and diarrhea.

The plant is easy to grow.

SLIDE 14 ### Indian Pipe, Ghost Plant
Monotropa uniflora L.

Few flowering plants appear on the forest floor in late summer. Most woodland plants have adapted to grow best in the brighter light and abundant moisture prevalent before tree leaves appear in spring. But in July and August one frequently may find the strange, fleshy stems, the vestigial, scalelike leaves, and the singular nodding, fleshy, ghostly white blooms of the Indian pipe. The plant is either a saprophyte, that is, deriving its nutrition from the digestion of decayed, organic debris in the soil, or it is an indirect parasite, a plant with a sort of fungal "slave" which connects the Indian pipe indirectly with the roots of a nearby living host from which it derives its nourishment. The exact nature of the plant's nutrition has not been resolved.

The petals of the solitary blooms are spoon-shaped, thickened, and fleshy, closely pressed to the organs within. After pollination, the nodding bloom slowly assumes an erect position. At the same time, the ovary enlarges and the dustlike, nearly microscopic seeds, adapted to transport by wind, develop in large numbers.

The blooming period is long. Fresh plants, although individually short-lived, can be found in a given district over a long period of the summer.

Most frequently the species grows in rich leaf mold in acid soils. It is quite indifferent to the type of forest cover and occurs in deciduous hardwoods and conifer humus. Because it is either saprophytic or parasitic, it can grow in exceptionally dark and humusy habitats, often where other flowering plants cannot survive. One of its least reported habitats is under dense thickets of black spruce, on the borders of spruce-tamarack sphagnum bogs. Here it is not unusual to find clumps of hundreds of stems.

The species ranges across North America from Newfoundland to Alaska and into the Deep South. A related species, pinesap (*Monotropa hypopithys* L.), with straw-yellow to reddish parts and a cluster of smaller flowers, has a similar range.

MEADOW AND STREAMBANK HABITATS

In upland areas, where streams meander and occasionally flood, there develop low wet areas, sometimes with trees overhead, sometimes more open, grassy, or shrubby. The influence of the flooding, the greater moisture, and the tendency to light levels more intense than those found in mature forest create growing conditions somewhat more varied than in the deciduous forest. Nearby fallow fields that are sunnier and drier may merge with the riverbank clearings, appearing loosely continuous with them.

In such habitats in the Northeast one finds not only specialized and exacting species in special niches but also plants rather tolerant of a variety of conditions which occur with certainty in moist old fields and along streams. These plants are discussed in this section.

Streambank and meadow habitats in this region, usually moist and somewhat cool, tend to have acid soils. Light is adequate or abundant, but competition for space is great. Therefore, one certain characteristic of the plant colonies growing in this situation is transience. Cardinal flower, fringed orchid, and bottle gentian cannot long compete with tree or shrub seedlings or with the dense stands of grass and rank herbs which develop here. But when suitable conditions exist, large showy colonies of reputed rarities often appear.

Plants from these localities usually grow well when cultivated in ordinary soils.

Wild Flowers of Meadow and Streambank Habitats

15. Skunk Cabbage (*Symplocarpus foetidus*)
16. Wild Iris (*Iris versicolor*)
17. Wild Columbine (*Aquilegia canadensis*)
18. Milkweed (*Asclepias spp.*)
19. Black-eyed Susan (*Rudbeckia hirta*)
20. Oxeye Daisy (*Chrysanthemum leucanthemum*)
21. Wood Lily (*Lilium philadelphicum*)
22. Fireweed (*Epilobium Angustifolium*)
23. Arrowhead (*Sagittaria latifolia*)
24. Jewelweed (*Impatiens capensis*)
25. Cardinal Flower (*Lobelia cardinalis*)
26. Bottle Gentian (*Gentiana andrewsii*)

SLIDE 15 **Skunk Cabbage**
Symplocarpus foetidus (L.) Nutt.

Everyone has heard the name "skunk cabbage," and it usually evokes a chuckle when mentioned. Yet how few nature lovers in some districts actually know this interesting plant! In many localities it is the first "wild flower" to bloom. It is not unusual for skunk cabbage to appear in wet seeps and about springs in mid-February.

A member of the arum family, like the jack-in-the-pulpit, it has the same basic flower structure: the spathe, a colored, thickened, modified leaf, sheaths the true flowering stalk or spadix. This "blossom," formed in a bud the previous summer, appears when mild sunny weather arrives in late winter or early spring. The spathe is usually mottled in shades of yellow, green, and dark maroon red. The knoblike spadix within is a strange flesh-pink color on the female or stigmatic surfaces. These are interspersed with the yellow, pollen-bearing anthers.

The flowers are pollinated by flies and beetles which hibernate over the winter and emerge to feed on warm sunny winter days. While the odor of the blooms may possibly suggest a skunk, it is far worse, especially at close range—a stench of rotting garbage rich in coffee grounds. This is an adaptive device, of course, to attract hungry, carrion seeking flies to the flowers. The true skunk odor which gives the plant its name is found in the jucies of the leaf or stem and becomes apparent only if the tissues become bruised.

Roots of the plant bear slightly contractile rings, and the roots expand or contract with changes in temperature, thus pushing the spathe up to attract insects in warmer hours, while pulling the spathe back against the relatively warm mud when freezing threatens.

The large, rhubarblike, light-yellow-green leaves appear after the blooms and are a conspicuous part of the wetland vegetation in the Northeast. Although not generally cultivated in wild gardens in this country, the plant is prized by Europeans for pool and streamside plantings.

Like the other arum species, the plant has been used as human food, but like its relatives, it contains irritating crystals and must be prepared properly. Bears are said to relish the plant and to devastate colonies when they find them.

SLIDE 16  ### Wild Iris, Blue Flag
Iris versicolor L. and *Iris virginica* L.

Two superficially similar large blue flags occur in the Eastern states. At first glance one is hard put to tell that they differ. But differences do occur in details of petal structure, seedpod, flower-scape height, and other technical features. In some districts they appear to intergrade.

Iris versicolor is the more generally northern species and is frequent in New York State. The bloom is the typical fleur-de-lis type and rather open.

As in orchids and amaryllis, the bases of the flower parts are fused around the ovary (inferior in position) and separate and somewhat flared beyond the ovary. Three segments, the outermost the sepals, spatulate-flared, reflex with a broad, distal lobe forming a more or less horizontal-drooping landing field for pollinating insects. The sepal expansion is marked with guidelines of white, yellow, and green. The three much narrower petals stand erect. In the irises, the long style branches of the ovary which bear petaloid wings over-arch the sepals. A thin, narrow stigmatic area of the style hangs rather closely above the sepal. Much as is the case with pollination in the orchids, the iris is pollinated when the insect visitor walks up the landing area provided by the sepal and scrapes against the stigma surface above, transferring any pollen the insect may be carrying. Large angular seed capsules develop quickly from successfully pollinated blooms.

The swamp irises characteristically form large clumps of lancelike leaves in or along ponds and streams and in low, wet meadows. The thick, creeping underground rhizomes compete vigorously with other lush swamp vegetation, and iris plants may persist for many years in a given location. The plants contain irisin, a dangerous poison which produces violent intestinal upsets.

A handsome plant, wild blue flag is easily cultivated, even in soils much drier than it occupies in the wild. Albino and especially dark forms occur.

SLIDE 17  ### Wild Columbine, "Honeysuckle"[1]
Aquilegia canadensis L.

Species of *Aquilegia* range across the entire Northern Hemisphere, and at maturity the plants vary from only 4 to 5 cm tall to over 8 dm in height. Colors range mostly in the blues or reds, although yellow and even deep-green- and blackish-flowered species occur.

The wild columbine of the Northeastern states and Canada is of medium height, with red to orange-red flowers. Columbine flowers are most distinctive in shape. Sepals and petals are colored alike, red shading to cream. The sepals spread, or radiate outward, appearing much like conventional petals. The somewhat liplike or scooped petals are erect but extended backward at their bases between the sepals into long, straight, or recurved hollow spurs, each with a somewhat bulbous nectary at the base. The numerous stamens and the stigma protrude as a cluster of organs from the center of the flower.

[1]The name "honeysuckle" is also applied locally to species of *Lonicera* and wild azalea (*Rhododendron* spp.).

It is the strange spurs on the flower which give the plant its Latin generic name, *Aquilegia*. The name derives, according to Fernald, from *aquila*, "the eagle," referring presumably to the resemblance of the curved petal spurs to the talons of an eagle. Others derive the name from *aqua*, "water," and *legere*, "to collect," referring to the nectar-filled spur.

Wild columbine or "honeysuckle" ranges from Maritime Canada southward to Florida, and westward to Texas in the South, and to Manitoba and Minnesota in the North.

Bumblebees eagerly visit blossoms of columbine. Often, when unable to reach the nectar by legitimate means, the bees bite holes in the spur and obtain the nectar prize from outside the blossom, apparently thwarting the adaptations intended to effect pollination. Butterflies and long-tongued moths also visit the plant, as do hummingbirds.

Columbine abounds in sandy woods clearings, dry fields, and on sunny rock outcrops or limestone cobbles. It is easily transplanted and comes readily from seed. The quality of flower varies considerably, and one interested in growing this or other wild flowers is well advised to select superior types for the garden. The plant can become somewhat weedy, so one ought at least to select a beautiful form.

The Milkweeds (Asclepias spp.)   There is a milkweed for almost every habitat. Representatives of this large genus grow in marshland, old fields, prairies, and woodlands. In all species, the individual flowers, born in clusters, are much alike in general appearance. The sepals (calyx) are small and borne below the ovary. The corolla has five lobes which are reflexed when the flower is open. Milkweed flowers possess another structure, a five-lobed crown or corona between corolla and stamens. There are five stamens. The ovary consists of two carpels, each of which develops into a large, fleshy pod. However, only a few pods develop from each umbellate cluster. The flattened, slightly winged seeds possess numerous white, hairy appendages which serve as a wind-borne parachute for seed dispersal.

SLIDE **18** ❀ ### Common Milkweed
Asclepias syriaca L.

This most familiar of all milkweeds grows in old fields and roadsides from New Brunswick to Saskatchewan and south to Georgia and Tennessee. A variety of the species grows westward into Kansas. Linnaeus bestowed the species name, *syriaca*, Latin indicating "from Syria," upon this plant in the mistaken belief that the specimens sent to him had come from that country. Because botanical rules of priority must be preserved to prevent nomenclatorial chaos, the misnomer stands.

This milkweed, with rather coarse stems up to 2 m high, spreads from deeply buried creeping rhizomes. The leaves, oblong to ovate and 1 to 2 dm long, are green above and whitish with tomentum below. Flowers appear in dense umbels. Two color forms occur in this species, one purplish or pink, one green with purple tinges. In either form the blooms are heavily and deliciously, even cloyingly, fragrant. Many insects eagerly visit the blooms. The flowers are followed by large, podlike follicles which are ovate and elongate-pointed toward the apex and have a silky soft surface bearing conical wartlike processes. The follicles split along one suture to liberate the familiar milkweed down and its attached seeds. The stems and fruit walls persist through the winter and often are gathered for use in winter bouquet arrangements.

During World War II, the silk from the seed follicles was gathered and used in life preservers as a substitute for kapok silk, a commodity from Asia and unobtainable in this country. The white milky juice of the stems of common milkweed contains latex.

Both the young shoots and the young fruits may be cooked as vegetables, but they are poisonous if eaten raw.

Common milkweed is a major food plant of the monarch butterfly. In late summer its black-, white-, and yellow-striped larvae or the exquisite green, gold-dotted chrysalids may frequently be found on the leaves of the plant.

SLIDE 19 ### Black-Eyed Susan
Rudbeckia hirta L.

Of all the native daisylike wild flowers, black-eyed Susan surely is the most widely known. It ranges over a wide area of North America from Massachusetts westward into the prairies, and southward to Georgia and Alabama. Due primarily to the conversion of forests to cultivated fields, we have greatly increased the available habitat for this plant in the East, and in recent times it has spread far beyond its original range.

Black-eyed Susan blooms over a long season, from early June until frost. It is among the earliest of the daisy-aster group to flower, and most people associate it with early summer. Locally abundant, its golden daisies present a beautiful sight when scattered in the angles of an old rail fence or among rocks and boulders along lakeshores or roadsides.

The basal leaves, somewhat rough and hairy, are a soft bluish green, about 15 to 20 cm long and 3 to 7 cm broad. Stem leaves are smaller but equally hairy. The branched flowering stems may reach 1 m in height, with each branch bearing a large and very showy flower head. The composite head has ten to twenty-five bright-yellow ray flowers, often with a blotch of darker color at the base of each ray, and a raised, prominently cone-shaped disk with densely packed, deep purple-brown, almost black florets. It is the disk which gives the plant its common name.

The plant is usually a biennial, making leaves and storing food the first year, then in the second producing flowers and seeds before it dies. Individual colonies, therefore, maybe transient, and it is characteristic of the species to vary in abundance locally from year to year.

Black-eyed Susan, if cultivated, is best utilized for naturalizing in moist meadows or grassy areas. It has been my experience that older plants of black-eyed Susan transplant with some difficulty. Therefore, it would probably be best for most gardeners to sow the seed in the spot where the flowers are needed.

SLIDE 20 ### Oxeye Daisy, Field Daisy, Marguerite
Chrysanthemum leucanthemum L.

Oxeye Daisy is a European plant which was early introduced into North America. Once here, it spread quickly and today may be found locally across the continent in the North, and locally southward in various forms to Florida, Kansas, and Texas. It blooms during June and July in fields and along roadsides in moist sandy or gravelly soils. Erect flowering stems 0.3 to 1 m tall bear numerous oblong or oblanceolate, regularly, coarsely toothed leaves. Each stalk at its summit has one or two white, yellow-centered daisies 4 to 6 cm across. As with all daisies and asters, what appears to be a single flower is in reality a complex, much shortened and modified branch with numerous flowers crowded into a dense central head which, with the surrounding petallike rays, appears to be one large blossom. Within the central area, the disk flowers bear no conspicuous petaloid parts but do contain the essential reproductive parts. The disk flowers in oxeye daisies are yellow. The adaptive economy of the daisy flower is that the visit of a single insect pollinates numerous blossoms and produces many seeds.

Wild daisies appear to be unpalatable to cattle, for when the plants invade pastures, the cattle graze around them and leave them alone unless no other choice is available. Such treatment favors a rapid buildup of the daisy population, for when the grasses are eaten, the newly available raw soil is quickly colonized by the daisy seedlings.

Over the northeast part of its range, oxeye daisy blooms are a favorite hiding place for the crab spider. This interesting arachnid does not use webs to trap insects. Instead, it hides in the center of a blossom and utilizes the flower's insect-attracting ability to lure insects, which then become the spider's prey. Since the spider is camouflaged and blends with the colors in the center of the flower, it is well hidden. Insect victims seem plentiful, for it is not unusual to find a spider feeding upon a beetle or butterfly and to find additonal corpses tucked away among the daisy's petals.

Oxeye daisies can be cultivated with comparative ease in an open, well-drained, not too fertile situation in the garden or in a meadow. If grown in too rich a soil, they lose some of their character. Large clumps should be divided every two years. One should be cautioned that this plant can seed aggressively into open ground.

Although the leaves of the plant have been used in Europe in salads, the odor of the leaf is strong. I cannot imagine its flavor would suit many Americans' tastes.

SLIDE 21 ✿ Wood Lily
Lilium philadelphicum L.

In early to mid-summer, wood lilies bloom in dry jack-pine woods, sandy open fields and meadows, in wild places along lakeshores, and in low, damp, marly meadows and bogs, over a very large part of Northeastern, Northern, and Northwestern North America. It is the only true lily with upright-facing flowers that occurs in the Northeast or North. The 2- to 6-dm stems usually grow singly and bear at their apex one to six blossoms in an open spreading umbel. The leaves develop either singly or in tiers of whorls along the stem, and the bulb, consisting of a cluster of fleshy, ricelike or kernellike modified leaves, is often buried deeply in humus or soil. The petals and sepals, colored alike, and with various blotches of yellow, green and dark maroon-black spots, usually are orange-red. Yellow-petaled forms, while rare, do occur in all districts where the plant grows.

Considered rare and a protected plant in some states, there are many areas where wood lilies abound. As with a great many so-called rare plants, the species really is not so rare as it is restricted to habitats exhibiting certain characteristics in vegetation development. It shuns shade and seems to thrive in specific types of disturbance. In dry, sandy, sterile soils, fire seems to contribute to the development of thriving colonies. Whether it is the opening of the woodland to light and air or the deposit of potash from burned trees which stimulates the plant is uncertain. The bog form often develops abundant colonies on the banks of ditches on roads cut through cedar and balsam swamps. Individual colonies develop and thrive for a few years, but when encroached upon and shaded by thickets or trees, they quickly wane. Too often, the disappearance of these plants is ascribed to picking rather than to the changes wrought by natural plant succession.

Although the Philadelphia lily is supposed to grow mostly on acid soils, the most vigorous plants and largest colonies I have seen are on thin, shallow soils over limestone cobble or bedrock in the upper Great Lakes regions, often in soils white with lime.

Cultivation of this wide-ranging lily ought to be easy, judging from its wide choice of habitats and its extensive distribution. But such is not the case. It resists transplanting. If it must be moved, make the attempt only when the plants are dormant. Mark the plants when they are in bloom, and return in the fall to dig up the bulbs. Plant the bulbs 10 to 15 cm deep in a soil mixture of sand and peat (do not plant them in ordinary loamy garden soil).

SLIDE 22 ✿ **Fireweed, Greater Willow Herb**
Epilobium angustifolium L.

Fireweed, one of the most spectacular wild flowers of the Northern Hemisphere, occurs circumboreally. Each plant produces one to twenty-five flowering stems which reach up to 2 m tall. Fireweed reaches its greatest vigor, highest abundance, largest flower size, and best colors in the cold Far North. No other flower attracts as much attention along the Alaska Highway or along other roads penetrating the subarctic wilderness.

The plants arise from stout perennial root crowns. The principal leaves are large, alternate, and thin-textured, green above and of a pale green-grey color below. Along the flowering raceme reduced leaflike bracts subtend each blossom. Flowers open slowly up the stem over a long period in summer, with bloom extending well over a month. The buds at first reflex gracefully, but they become more erect as the blooms open. The blooms have a somewhat squarish appearance. Each bears four rather large petals, usually magenta but occasionally pink or white, which open relatively flat. The style is distinctively declined.

The willowlike leaf of this and related species gives the genus the name "willow herb." The name "fireweed" derives from the tendency of this species to be the first large herb to appear after forest fires devastate the spruce woods of the North. Along the Alaska Highway, I have seen thousands of acres of fireweed carpeting recent burns, the plants growing almost to the exclusion of other vegetation. But such luxuriance is short-lived, for the plants do not compete well with the inevitably invading grasses and shrubs, and colonies gradually dwindle as competition increases. Any form of soil disturbance stimulates the seeds, apparently, for roadscraping or bulldozing within the fireweed's range is invariably followed by development of colonies of the plant on the disturbed surface.

In spite of its extraordinary beauty and abundance in certain regions, and its wide distribution, the plant rarely is cultivated. It is apparently very difficult to transplant; I have succeeded only once, with an albino form. Seed is fine and attached to cottony fluff for air transport. One wild-flower grower suggests scattering or planting seeds on raw soil and then covering the area with straw, which is burned to simulate the effects of wildfires, which favor development of large, lush colonies.

SLIDE 23 🌸 **Arrowhead, Swamp Potato**

Sagittaria latifolia Willd.

In the shallow waters of marshes and small lakes and in the muds and sands of sluggish streams grow the arrowheads. These distinctive plants have broad or narrow arrow-shaped leaves arising from subterranean rootstocks. Most species are under 6 dm tall. In many species the leaves can be polymorphic, with a single colony including plants with broad blades as well as others with narrow, slender ones. Arrowheads may also produce purely aquatic, strap-shaped, recurved leaves below the surface of shallow waters. Many of these aquatic forms find wide use as aerators in aquaria.

In summer the flower cluster, a raceme, arises, bearing flowers usually in whorls of threes. The raceme continues to elongate and produce flowers into autumn. Each flower may be of either or both sexes. The most conspicuous features of the blossom are the three rather large, white, somewhat crinkled, 1- to 2-cm-long petals and the large cluster of separate ovaries borne in green, globose head.

With the approach of autumn, the plants produce fleshy tubers at tbe ends of long subterranean runners, often some distance from the parent plant. These edible tubers, much sought after by ducks and waterfowl, make the plant a desirable aid in attracting wild water birds. The Indians of North America used the tubers for food, utilizing them much as we do potatoes. Since the buried tubers were difficult to locate, many Indians obtained their supply by raiding food caches assembled by muskrats. Lewis and Clark noted the food value of the plant. But modern would-be natural-food gatherers should first know the plant exactly, for the arrowlike leaves resemble also those of arrow arum and others with dangerous properties.

SLIDE 24 🌸 **Jewelweed, Touch-Me-Not**

Impatiens capensis Meerb.

Plants of this genus, although often somewhat weedy in growth habit, have most distinctive flowers. In the native American species, all annuals, three two-lobed petals and three sepals unite into a trumpet-shaped, somewhat two-lipped bloom. The blossom hangs from a slender pedicel. Color of the flower usually is light orange with much deeper orange-red spots, although other color forms occur. Hummingbirds eagerly visit the flowers, as do hawk moths, and effect pollination. The fleshy, spindle-shaped capsule, about 2 cm long, still green when the seeds ripen, splits violently along two sutures when touched near its tip, scattering seed over a considerable distance. It is this explosive behavior of the ripe seed capsules which gives to the plant the name "touch-me-not." Once aware of its method of seed dispersal, children and adults alike delight in triggering the capsule release. The two fleshy outer halves of the capsule coil up into a mealy spiral of tissue upon discharge of seeds.

The rangy, succulent, almost translucent stems of jewelweed bear swollen joints (nodes) and soft, pale bluish-green to green leaves covered with a faint whitish bloom. The juices of the stem are said to dry up the blisters and relieve the irritation of poison ivy. But the stems are also reported to be harmful when ingested by stock animals.

Touch-me-not is one of the most familiar plants of wet places, springy areas, marsh borders, and swampy woods and ditches, where it often grows in great abundance, especially in partial shade. The broad, almost rectangular cotyledons of germinating seedlings are familiar sights in the spring woodland. The observant naturalist will often find a dense cluster of dozens or even hundreds of seedlings springing from one spot in the ground, so crowded that the plants could not possibly all survive. Such concentrations of seedlings mark the location of a mouse's forgotten seed cache.

Orange jewelweed ranges across most of the North American continent from Newfoundland and Quebec to Saskatchewan and southward to South Carolina, Alabama, and Oklahoma.

SLIDE 25 ## Cardinal Flower

Lobelia cardinalis L.

There is no more spectacularly colorful stately summertime flower than cardinal flower. The great spikes of rich deep red emblazen streambanks, ditches, low floodplain woods, meadows, and streams in late July and August. Vigorous individuals, often a meter or more in height, usually produce several flowering stems. Although they are closely related to the bluebells (*Campanula* spp.), the relationship is not at first apparent when one examines the irregular scarlet bloom. Cardinal flower bears numerous flowers on short pedicels along the tall spike. Above the sepals, each blossom is at first tubular and then becomes more or less divided into two lips, the upper consisting of two rather erect petal lobes and the lower lip with three spreading lobes. From between the lobes extend the stamens and stigma, forming a compact, columnar cluster. Two of the anthers are conspicuously white-bearded. At the base of this column of organs and at the base of the three lower petal lobes is an opening that leads to the nectar supply. The flower is pollinated by hummingbirds and hummingbird (sphinx) moths. When the hummingbird hovers at the bright bloom and approaches the opening for nectar, its beak, bearing pollen from flowers visited earlier, brushes against the stigma and thus effects pollination. When the bird applies pressure to the anthers as it feeds, pollen oozes from the open anther ends, dusting a fresh supply of pollen over the bird's beak to be carried to another cardinal flower in cross-pollination.

As in many hummingbird-pollinated flowers, there is little or no fragrance in the bloom. Birds search food by sight and have a poorly developed sense of smell. Consequently adaptation of the plant to attract its pollinator has gone in the direction of brilliant color.

It is normal for cardinal flower colonies to be short-lived in a given spot. The plant does not compete well with weedy vegetation. Typically it invades low, wet, raw soils, muddy sandbars in streams, and recently cleaned-out ditches. Germination in such situations is commonly abundant and plants may mature in one season in favorable conditions. In a year or two, a very large colony can develop. But invariably, unless the raw situation is renewed by new flooding or other disturbances, the changes wrought by accumulated debris, humus, and competition with other invading plants for light gradually weaken and destroy the cardinal flower plants. Cardinal flower depends upon continued opening of newly exposed soil for colonization as older colonies dwindle. In road construction, ditching, and clearing of some types of swamps, ideal conditions are sometimes temporarily produced and there is suitable habitat for a brief flourishing of enormous colonies of these scarlet lobelias.

Cardinal flower may be grown relatively easily in a moderately rich, permanently moist soil in open shade, but only if one keeps weeds and other plants from encroaching upon the base of the plant. But with excessive crowding in the garden, as in the wild, it cannot compete and soon succumbs. Besides reproducing by seeds, cardinal flower may be propagated by bending flowering stems to the ground and heaping clumps of soil over the buds of the joints or nodes. In time plantlets form at the nodes.

The species ranges from Quebec to Minnesota and southward to Florida and eastern Texas. From Missouri to Texas south and westward ranges a similar but slenderer species.

Look for cardinal flower in low woods along upland streams where water stands late in springtime. It frequently grows in the the company of sensitive fern (*Onoclea*), purple-fringed orchid, and tubercled orchid. Also search on muddy bars in trout streams. Sometimes attractive white or pale rose-pink mutants occur.

Although cardinal flower appears on protected lists of some states, it is seldom truly rare. Rather, as noted, its colonies constantly wax and wane in a given spot. This has led some to assume incorrectly that its disappearance on these sites resulted from human depredation. Like all but the most aggressive weeds, it does shrink from the excessive habitat destruction caused by draining, soil moving, and land development.

SLIDE 26

Bottle Gentian, Closed Gentian
Gentiana andrewsii Griesb.

This rather tall sometimes rather coarse gentian may be one of the best known American wild flowers. It blooms late in the year when few flowers other than small asters bloom. The shape of its blooms, rather like the old-fashioned Christmas-tree bulbs, catch the eye. The two to five flowering stems arise from a perennial and long-lived root to a height of 3 to 8 dm. Flowers appear in clusters at the end of the stem and often in the axils of leafy involucres near the summit. Corolla color ranges from a beautiful, clear, deep sky blue to some rather violet-purple shades, often streaked with green tones. The much pleated and folded corolla appears more like a bud than a fully developed flower. Pollination is effected, at least in the large colonies in my meadow, by large bumblebees which alight upon the platformlike clusters of leaves immediately below the flowers. Standing upon its hind legs, the bee barely reaches to the apex of the flower "bottle." It inserts its front legs into the tip of the bloom and pushes the pleated flower segment apart. With this pressure, the bloom springs open and the bee dives in. But the moment the pressure on the corolla is released the flower snaps back to its "closed" position with the bee trapped inside. The alarmed bee struggles to free itself; in so doing it dusts pollen upon the stigma of the bloom, and at the same time becomes dusted with more pollen for another flower.

Closed gentian is at home in a variety of habitats. It is best developed in a sandy loam with permanent moisture and grows commonly along small streams, in open woods, and in damp meadows. Like cardinal flower, it may actually become abundant in such artificial habitats as cleaned-out ditches.

It is native in most of the area from Quebec to Manitoba and southward to the uplands of Georgia and Arkansas, and varies from common to rare in the various districts.

Bottle gentians may be cultivated in almost any soil, even if drier than in its wild habitat. But it does not transplant easily as a large plant. The easiest method of culture, in suitable meadow habitats, is merely to collect and scatter the seed in an open, moist spot that is not too weedy. Gentians will appear in bloom in two or three seasons. Seed may also be sown in flats and the small seedlings set out.

Albino flowers and color variations in blues occur not too rarely and many are desirable horticulturally. If a plant must be collected and transplanted from the wild instead of grown from seed, dig it in a manner to preserve the soil about its roots and move a whole sod.

Several related and rather similar species of gentian also grow within the range covered by this book, but none is common except the bottle gentian.

NORTHERN CONIFEROUS FOREST AND SPRUCE-TAMARACK BOG

Some habitats are ecologically unique. The soil, climate, and moisture conditions limit the life present to those species tolerant of only that one environment. Some habitats are not so exclusive. Conditions within them overlap enough with those of other seemingly different but actually similar habitats that some of the species typical of one can also flourish at least in microenvironments within others. Where these related habitats interconnect geographically, plant species can often spread across very large areas. So it is with many plants of the Northern coniferous forests and spruce-tamarack boglands. Species that New Englanders consider typical of their pinewoods occur also on mountaintop forests as far south as North Carolina as well as across the expanse of the boreal forests of Canada and Alaska, at high elevations in the Rocky and Sierra Nevada Mountains, and across Eurasia as well. While environmental conditions may at first seem very different on a Carolina mountaintop, in a Connecticut pinewoods, and in the forests and bogs of Alaska, the factors affecting plant growth are surprisingly similar as they are met in these diverse regions.

Because of deep shade or the constant evaporation of the high water table, soils throughout the coniferous forests and bogs remain cooler in summer and relatively warmer in winter than do surrounding, drier, more exposed soils. Lack of available oxygen in the wet soils, or the acidity of the conifer-needle mulch, or both, inhibit decay of the accumulated plant debris. A peaty humus, therefore, builds up to great depths. The surface stratum is almost pure organic duff. Its intensely acid reaction tends to insulate the soil chemically from the surrounding mineral subsoils, so that nutrients only a few feet away from the roots of the plants may be totally unavailable to them.

Many species of coniferous forest and bog habitats, therefore, have developed similar requirements for soil acidity, temperature, and humus, or for special soil-fungus partnerships which enable them to obtain required nutrients in spite of the complex soil chemistry.

Sodden sphagnum peat bogs may seem quite unlike drier coniferous forests at first, but the differences are superficial. Surprisingly, few plants characteristic of our spruce-tamarack bogs grow in these bogs because of a need for large amounts of water. Some true hydrophytes occur, of course, but most of the orchids, blueberries, cranberries, and other heath plants are restricted to bogs because of their soil or temperature requirements, as mentioned above. When these conditions are met in places other than wet-bog cover, these plants may occur there also. This accounts for the great amount of overlap of species between coniferous forest, pine barren, boreal forest, and bog.

Plants of the open bog, in addition to requiring acid humus soil, generally demand full sunlight. Some need a raw, open substrate free from competing plants. The great beds of sphagnum moss may meet their moisture and acidity requirements and at the same time provide them with the competition-free situation they need.

One of the botanical charms of a bog is the chance to discover rarities not generally found elsewhere in the region. The rarities may be Northern species demanding cold soil temperatures and surviving in the bogs as Ice Age relicts because the bog alone meets soil and temperature needs. Likewise, Southern species may extend north of their general distributional limits because soil conditions in Northern bogs are similar to those of wet-sand habitats of the South. Since percolating water in bogs prevents deep freezing or very low soil temperatures over the long winter, Southern species often can live in the northerly bog but would perish in the more severe winter condition of adjacent upland.

Truly, plants of the northeastern bogs have delicate and complex relationships with their environment. Two species growing in proximity may grow there for vastly different ecological reasons. Therefore, to grow them under garden conditions may prove difficult without knowing those reasons. Unless one is willing to expend a special effort to understand and meet the requirements, one should not attempt their cultivation.

Wild Flowers of the Northern Coniferous Forest and Spruce-Tamarack Bog

27. Trailing Arbutus (*Epigaea repens*)
28. Wild Lily of the Valley (*Maianthemum canadense*)
29. Pink Lady's-Slipper (*Cypripedium acaule*)
30. Yellow Bead Lily (*Clintonia borealis*)
31. Painted Trillium (*Trillium undulatum*)
32. Ground Dogwood (*Cornus canadensis*)
33. Showy Lady's-Slipper (*Cypripedium reginae*)

Wild Flowers of the Open Peat Bog

34. Buckbean (*Menyanthes trifoliata*)
35. Arethusa (*Arethusa bulbosa*)
36. Northern Pitcher Plant (*Sarracenia purpurea*)
37. Grass Pink (*Calopogon tuberosus*)
38. Rose Pogonia (*Pogonia ophioglossoides*)
39. Cow Lily (*Nuphar* spp.)
40. White Fringed Orchid (*Habenaria blephariglottis*)

SLIDE 27 **Trailing Arbutus, Mayflower**
Epigaea repens L.

In earliest spring, from late March to May, depending upon latitude and habitat, trailing arbutus comes into bloom. Its Latin name, *Epigaea,* translates "upon the ground." Truly this name is appropriate, for this almost woody plant forms a creeping mat of rather large, rough, oval leaves and stems that root here and there through the sandy peat or mosses in which it grows. Large clusters of flower buds that appeared in the previous autumn terminate the branches. With early spring warming, the dainty clusters of flowers appear.

The corolla of united petals is tubular but expanded and flattened at the apex into five lobes. Most plants produce white or very faintly pink petals, but occasional individuals have very dark, rosy pink blossoms of especial beauty. Part of the charm of the plant lies in the earliness of its bloom and its appearance in usually rather austere habitats. But a very large part of the plant's charm lies in the deliciously spicy fragrance of the delicate flowers.

Mayflower is one of the wild flowers better known to those who are not particularly interested in flowers. It enjoys a legendary reputation. Until it was protected by law in many places, rural people gathered nosegays of these plants to sell in local markets. Mayflower is generally reputed to have been made rare by such activities. Many authors cite its trailing habit and how tearing it up for bouquets has destroyed the plants in many districts. Although many plants have undoubtedly perished in this manner, a major cause of local disappearance is natural plant succession. Arbutus thrives best in bright light. After forest fires, road-building, or other habitat disturbance, it frequently seeds abundantly into moss beds on the scarred, sterile, acid soils. For a period of years such colonies thrive, but as the soil recovers and shrubs and trees mature, arbutus wanes, a victim more often of the encroaching shade than of the flower pickers so often blamed.

The seeds ripen in a globular, many-seeded capsule, just at the time when wild strawberries ripen in the same districts. Those desiring to grow arbutus can collect seed and scatter it in peaty sands, on rotten logs, or in peat pots. The seeds germinate easily but the seedlings take a year or more to reach transplanting size. Transplanting sods of the plant can be done, but seldom successfully unless one almost exactly duplicates the soil from which the clump was taken. Rooted cuttings are reputed to be the most satisfactory state for introduction into the garden. Cuttings may be easily rooted on a small scale by inserting a number of them in damp live sphagnum in a gallon jar which is covered and placed in strong north light. The cuttings will take several months to root.

Trailing arbutus occurs in the acid soils of many different habitats over much of the Eastern United States and Canada, from Newfoundland to Florida and Mississippi. In the North it grows from Labrador to Saskatchewan. In the Blue Ridge Mountains it is not uncommon to find the plant growing abundantly on the wet, seepy faces of sandstone cliffs, while to the north, although occurring in open sandy pine and oak barrens, it often grows on rotting logs in old cedar-balsam fir swamps.

As with many of our trilliums, orchids, and azaleas, there is a closely related species of arbutus in Japan.

SLIDE 28 **Wild Lily of the Valley, Canada Mayflower**
Maianthemum canadense Desf.

In spite of its name, this plant bears only a remote resemblance to the garden lily of the valley. Immature plants produce a single, cordate leaf of glossy bright apple green. The often zigzag flowering stalks bear two or three leaves and rise to 5 to 18 cm above the slender, creeping, perennial rootstalks. Glabrous stem leaves, usually 2 to 10 cm long and 2 to 5 cm broad, lightly clasp the stem. The numerous, tiny, four-parted white blossoms form a dense spikelike terminal raceme. Fleshy berries, at first pearly green, then red-flecked, and finally deep translucent red and juicy, follow the blooms. The red berries frequently persist into the winter. They are cathartic and possibly dangerous if eaten.

Although *Maianthemum canadense* is found in cool, acid, humusy coniferous woods and bogs in our region, thus suggesting affinity with boreal species, it has a distribution pattern resembling that of the many deciduous forest plants of the Eastern United States. It ranges from Newfoundland and Manitoba southward to Georgia in the mountains. In the Northeast, it is common in subalpine habitats and on hummocks and rotted logs in bogs as well as in a variety of acid-soil woodlands and thickets.

Canada mayflower may be cultivated with ease in a sandy humus. Pieces of creeping rhizome may be planted, or sods may be dug from the wild and set in place. Given some freedom from weeds, the plants usually spread quickly. It is a characteristic of the plant in some areas to jump about, thriving in one spot for a period and then dwindling. Once established in a woodland or wild garden, however, it seldom disappears completely. It is well worthy of cultivation, is not rare in most districts, and, so far as I am aware, is not a protected plant.

SLIDE 29 ✿ **Pink Lady's-Slipper, Moccasin Flower, Whippoorwill's-Shoe**
Cypripedium acaule Ait.

The pink lady's-slipper grows over a large part of Northeastern North America and in a wide variety of habitats within its range. All of its habitats have one attribute in common: intensely acid soil. The plant frequently appears in great abundance locally. One might expect, therefore, that the species could be cultivated easily. Such is not the case. Of all the cypripedia, this is the most difficult native to grow. Many people have reported success, but in most cases, if one investigates, one finds that the "success" represents a clump dug one season which appeared and flowered the next. All the lady's slippers make next season's leaves and flowers during the present growing season; they remain as a large dormant bud on the rhizome. This bud can coast on stored food and develop and bloom in the spring. But most plants that are transplanted to the wrong conditions succumb to soil fungi or other ailments after spring bloom of the season following transplanting. The test of success with pink lady's-slippers is the appearance and flowering of a plant over a period of several seasons.

Moccasin flower seems completely tolerant of the range of temperatures in North America, for it grows in upland Georgia and Alabama where summer temperatures scorch the earth, and in subarctic Manitoba and even near Great Bear Lake where temperatures in the soil seldom get above the high forties! It grows in deep humus, pine needles, rich beds of sphagnum moss, and also in nearly pure, infertile granite sands.

Like most terrestrial orchids, the various lady's slippers grow in association with soil fungi in a partnership arrangement (symbiosis). This association starts when the seed germinates. In the orchids, there is no preformed embryo or food supply in the seed, and the orchid seed depends upon the fungus to aid in germination. Certain species of soil fungi attack the mass of cells which comprise the orchid seed, digesting outer cells and converting their food materials to sugars. These sugars, if available to the orchid seed, stimulate growth. In a soil suitably acid and sterile, the balance between the fungus's growth and the orchid seed's growth is struck, the fungus growth is held in check, and digestion on the outside of the orchid seed cell mass proceeds slowly enough so that the inner cells, utilizing released sugar quickly, organize to form an embryo and commence growth instead of being consumed. The fungus becomes associated with the orchid roots for the life of the orchid. Botanists consider the relationship truly symbiotic, each organism physiologically aiding the other.

In flower structure, moccasin flowers differ somewhat from the other lady's slippers. Instead of an herbaceous stem bearing three to five leaves arising from the subterranean rhizome and root system, two leaves arise directly from the rhizome. A naked flower scape ascending between the leaves bears first a leaflike bract and ovary, then the remarkable blossom. Sepals and all petals but one are small, strap-shaped, relatively inconspicuous, and either dark purplish brown or green. The outstanding feature of the flower is the great, pendulous pouch or slipper, a modified petal. Instead of being formed into the typical lady's-slipper cup, it is split down the full length of the upper side with the edges of the split folded inward, so that the folds form two lengthwise ridges. The base color of the pouch is usually a delicate pink but ranges from pure white in albinos through rose tones to dark reddish purple.

As in all species of lady's slipper, the pollination devices of the lip are similar. The visiting insect enters the slit opening in the lip. Because of the form of the cleft and the tension upon its margins on the inside, the insect cannot usually leave as it enters. Hairs, nectaries, and often translucent windows lead the insect up the back of the floor of the lip under the staminode, stigma, and finally pollen-bearing anthers at the point of lip attachment. If the insect carries pollen from another moccasin flower, it must first crawl under the stigma, to which pollen is thus transferred. As the insect leaves the bloom, it triggers dispersal of pollen from the present flower to its back, which is then carried to another bloom. Cross-pollination rather than self-pollination is almost assured. Sometimes, however, the efficiency of this mechanism is thwarted by a large bumblebee which, impatient with the usual exit procedure simply chews a hole in the blooms and leaves by its own route.

Far the most difficult lady's slipper to cultivate, moccasin flowers are generally protected plants.

SLIDE 30 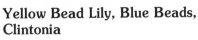 **Yellow Bead Lily, Blue Beads, Clintonia**

Clintonia borealis (Ait.) Raf.

Clintonia grows in a variety of cool, shaded, humusy habitats across eastern boreal America from Newfoundland and Laborador to Manitoba, and southward through Minnesota and the Lakes states to southern New England. Along the higher Appalachian mountain chains it extends south to Georgia and Tennessee. Its large, rather fleshy cluster of two to four somewhat boat-shaped leaves borne from an underground, creeping rhizome are a familiar sight to all who tramp the evergreen woods and bogs. A 2- to 3-dm-tall flower scape bears two to eight greenish yellow or lemon-colored blossoms typical in structure of the lily family. The floral segments, all alike in texture and color, but with slightly spreading tips and downy outsides are, 2 to 3 cm long and nod slightly. Individual plants vary in the quality and size of their blooms. When a flower is pollinated, the floral segments become thin-textured and shrivel quickly. Rather large, dark blue, firm berries follow the not-too-showy blooms in mid-summer. The beadlike berries are quite conspicuous and attractive but have been described by many authors as poisonous.

Like many plants of the boreal forests, this species is adapted to cool summer temperatures and cannot tolerate heating of the soil. Lumbering, transplanting to gardens, or any change which exposes the plants to much intense sunlight or warming results in reduction in size and vigor of the plant. Yet in the Far North, where even in sunlight the soils remain cool, one may find great colonies of the plant in open, fully exposed situations.

Bluebead lily is very difficult to transplant and establish. It requires deep, acid humus and moisture, and should be given nearly full shade. Large sods dug carefully and replanted intact in a suitable spot offer the best chance for success. For most persons, it is perhaps best to enjoy the charm of this plant in the wild and not attempt to grow it.

Clintonia enjoys a rather singular distinction. Probably no other plant has had its leaves mistaken more often for those of orchids. It grows in orchid habitats, often with orchid companions, and its leaves look very much like cypripedium and some habenaria leaves. If one is confronted with a perplexing set of monocot leaves and it is important to determine if it is an orchid or clintonia, one may quickly tell by examining the lateral leaf margins carefully, with a hand lens if necessary. If the margins are softly hairy, it is not an orchid and probably is clintonia. Young leaves may also resemble those of bog false Solomon's seal, with which it often grows.

The flowers of clintonia attract vast numbers of yellow swallowtail butterflies, which feed on the bloom's nectar.

SLIDE 31 ## Painted Trillium
Trillium undulatum Willd.

No other trillium species is more closely associated with deeply shaded woodland or mountain fastness than the painted trillium. It is restricted to cool and rather intensely acid soil, and is a plant essentially of Northeastern North America. It ranges from the Gaspé Peninsula and Quebec westward into the eastern Great Lakes region. Although it has been reported to occur as far west as Manitoba, I have seen no herbarium specimens collected west of North Bay, Ontario. Southward, it occurs locally in New England, New York, and New Jersey westward into the eastern counties of Michigan and southward locally along the mountains from Pennsylvania to Georgia. The plant is often associated with rhododendron and azalea thickets, but it can grow under hemlock and white pine, in red maple and aspen woods, or in peaty bog margins if soils are not too wet. In its most favored habitats, a deep layer of brown acid humus overlies a white quartz-sand subsoil. The trillium's rhizomes usually grow with the upper part covered with 4 to 8 inches of acid duff and with the roots extending below the rhizome into the damp, relatively pure sand. In our region, at least, the plant demands deep summer shade.

The growth pattern differs from that of most trilliums. This plant is late to appear above ground and blooms when other trillium species in the same district are rapidly fading or long finished. One could almost say the plant appears above ground in bloom, so quickly does the bud open over the still small and bronzy foliage. But all parts quickly expand so that today's tiny plant may be tomorrow's very large and showy one—if the bloom is not pollinated. When development proceeds for several days without pollination, the plant attains a height of up to 5 dm and its distinctly petioled, ovate and long-acuminate leaves may be over 15 cm broad. The single, white, three-petaled flower may be up to 5 to 6 cm across and very showy. When pollinated before full expansion has taken place, however, the petals respond to a ripening hormone liberated by the pollen and become transparent and dull. Growth then ceases and within a day or so the petals shrivel and die.

The plant is called "painted trillium" because of the prominent V-shaped red blotch and stripes near the base of each petal. These markings probably act as guidelines to insect pollinators and certainly do add interest and highlights to the beauty of the blossom.

An oval, obscurely three-angled berry follows the flower. In this species the fruit is held erect, is prominent, and is a rich scarlet when ripe. Once colored up, it persists only a day or two on the plant. Although self-deciduous, the berry is much sought after by birds and ants, which seldom allow it to remain on the plant even for its short natural ripening span.

Painted trillium is a protected plant in many states, and rightly so. It is locally rare, difficult of cultivation, short-lived under garden conditions, and of all trilliums the most dependent upon undisturbed, primeval forest conditions. It should be enjoyed only in the wild. If cultivation is a must, then stock should be obtained from a dependable wild-flower nursery and not from wild colonies.

SLIDE 32 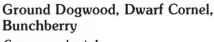 **Ground Dogwood, Dwarf Cornel, Bunchberry**
Cornus canadensis L.

Ground dogwood grows over a very large part of boreal North America, from Greenland and Newfoundland to central Alaska and rather commonly southward wherever cool, rather moist coniferous forests develop. In the mountains it extends well to the south where cool temperatures prevail. In the Canadian Northwest, Yukon, and Alaska, it is sometimes the most abundant of all ground-cover plants and carpets thousands of square miles of mixed birch and spruce forest. Over its range it grows with many rare and beautiful wild flowers. Such companion plants include *Clintonia, Goodyera* (rattlesnake plantains), tway-blades, lady's slippers, sweet violets, and fringed polygalas.

Dwarf cornel is a leathery herbaceous plant which spreads to form dense colonies by underground runners. On stems of 0.5 to 2 dm (but usually 1 to 1.5 dm) several tiers of opposite leaves appear. The lower are small and obscure, the upper ones larger, 2 to 9 cm long, ovate-oblong to rhombic, unequal in size, with prominent, pinnate veins, and appearing falsely to be borne in a whorl. The leaves are semi-evergreen, and if protected by a heavy cover of snow are completely evergreen. In autumn, they often take on beautiful deep maroon-bronze tones.

What appears at first to be a single, four-petaled flower is in fact more complex. The four "petals" are in reality elliptic to round-ovate, creamy white bracts (modified leaves) surrounding and subtending a tight head (cyme) of minute, four-petaled, greenish or maroon-tipped flowers. Large, fleshy, but insipid bright-red fruits commonly called "berries" follow the tiny flower in late summer. In reality the fruits are drupes, that is, fruits with a hard pit or stone surrounding the true seed and covered with flesh without, as in a peach or plum. Although edible, the berries are dry and tasteless.

This is one of the most popular wild flowers of the cool North. It is not an easy plant to grow. Sods may be transplanted into any sandy-acid humus and the plants may persist for years, but they bloom sparsely unless soil temperatures fall within suitable ranges.

SLIDE 33 Showy Lady's-Slipper, Queen's Lady Slipper
Cypripedium reginae Walt.

Few plants rival the showy lady's-slipper for its stately beauty or for the beauty of its habitat. Standing 3 to 8 dm tall and usually forming loose clumps, each plant bears from one to three flowers. Each blossom has an enormous, rounded, concave, delicately ribbed white dorsal sepal 3 to 4 cm in diameter. Each spreading white petal reaches over 3 cm in length and is 1 to 1.5 cm broad. The lip dominates the blossom with its much-ribbed and inflated, subglobose pouch, 3 to 5 cm long and broad. Various tones or shades of pink or rose color the outside of the slipper, with the coloring most intense near the opening at the top. Inside, the color is suffused throughout and shows small rows of purplish dots. Bees pollinate the flower much in the same manner as that described for the pink lady's-slipper.

A rather large, dark green, leafy bract subtends each blossom and has the effect of setting off the color of the blossom. The hairy stems produce three to five quite large, ovate, strongly ribbed leaves. The hairs of both stem and leaf cause a serious skin irritation in susceptible persons.

Showy lady's-slipper ranges, or did range, from Newfoundland southward very locally into Pennsylvania and to the mountains of Georgia, and westward through the Great Lakes regions to Minnesota and Manitoba. It is the state flower of Minnesota. Showy lady's-slipper blooms in June and July in the North.

A lover of "wet feet," the plant grows at its best in sodden, mossy glades in cedar-balsam or tamarack swamps. In such situations, light is critical. The lady's-slipper cannot tolerate dense shade; hence populations build up in glades, along trails, and in windfall clearings. The late Prof. Waterman suggested that overgrazing by the whitetail deer in their wintering yards in cedar swamps created ideal habitat. At any rate, the largest colonies, often with thousands of plants, develop in old, overbrowsed deeryards and persist there until swarms of balsam-fir seedlings overtop the orchid and shade it to death.

Despite much that has been written to the contrary, showy lady's-slipper may be easily cultivated by a variety of methods in light shade in a rich neutral to slightly acid muck soil kept well watered in summer. It must not be fertilized with mineral fertilizers, and it is best mulched lightly in winter. Field mice and meadow voles voraciously attack the winter buds which push to the surface of the soil in autumn.

Because the plant is protected in most areas, it ought not to be collected in the wild. Reliable wild-flower nurseries offer propagations and divisions of acclimated stock.

Like those of all lady's slippers and many other orchids, the roots of the queen's lady slipper emit a strong, agreeable, characteristic odor. At least part of this odor is due to the compound vanillin, the essential ingredient in vanilla flavoring. Vanilla, incidentally, is just about the only important food product produced in the entire orchid family, although orchids constitute one of the largest families of flowering plants. Deer apparently appreciate vanilla flavoring, for it is common to find the developing sprouts or mature plants of lady's slippers heavily and selectively grazed.

SLIDE 34 ❧ Buckbean, Bogbean
Menyanthes trifoliata L.

Few would recognize that the clustered, white, hoary and snowflakelike blooms of buckbean are those of a member of the gentian family. Yet that is exactly the relationship of the plant. Buckbean grows in the Northern Hemisphere in cold bogs, on remote arctic lakeshores, and in tundra pools. The common-name reference to bean alludes to the three-parted compound leaves which vaguely resemble those of the garden pea or bean plant. The plant spreads from a creeping rootstock sheathed by the leaf bases and develops large colonies.

The flower raceme is borne on a stalk often 1 to 3 dm high, though sometimes shorter, with plants in open water appearing to bloom most heavily. Each flower is 1 to 3 cm across, the united petals carried rather flatly. The striking feature of the flower is the corolla, the upper surface of which is snow white and heavily bearded with frostlike processes. Sometimes the petal or beard tips are touched with dark maroon.

Buckbean is one of the earliest of wild flowers in the cold bogland to bloom, reaching its peak in favored habitats in mid-May. By the first week in June it is very difficult to find a flowering plant in good condition.

Few wild-flower enthusiasts properly appreciate the beauty of this plant, perhaps because it prefers remote, cold, and very wet bogs, and blooms so early in the year. Yet it can be grown in bog gardens, or even in a wooden tub on a terrace. The foliage is attractive and the flowers exquisite.

Fernald and Kinsey, in their book *Edible Wild Plants of Eastern North America*, report that buckbean contains a bitter principle that is characteristic of the gentian family. They report, nevertheless, that when dried the plant is used by Laplanders and Finns to make famine-bread. Linnaeus described the bread as nutritious but thoroughly unpalatable.

SLIDE 35 ❧ Arethusa, Dragon's-Mouth
Arethusa bulbosa L.

Few more delicately beautiful plants occur anywhere than this delightful diminutive orchid. The flower scape at blooming time appears naked, for the single grasslike leaf sheaths the base of the stem and develops to full size only after blooming is over. This habit emphasizes and enhances the showiness of the bloom. The stem arises from a tiny bulblike corm nestled loosely in the sphagnum moss of remote peat bogs or the sandy peat of low Northern meadows and beaches The single, rich magenta-pink flower is striking in form. Morris and Eames in their classic book *Our Wild Orchids* compare the blossom to a quaint wild beast, startled, with ears pricked and mouth agape, alert for some half-heard sound. It is an apt allusion.

Although considered generally rare, arethusa can be locally abundant, especially in sphagnum bogs of the Far North. It does not appear to be long-lived, or if it is, it seldom survives the wintertime predation of mice upon its food-laden bulbs, as even remote populations fluctuate greatly. Since this plant, like many orchids, produces vanillin in its tissues, and its roots emit the odor of vanilla, it may be this flavoring which attracts the mice.

Arethusa blooms in June and July. Bumblebees pollinate the plants, but seed is not often set. Growing as it so often does in Northern sphagnum bogs, Arethusa could not have more interesting plant companions. Orchid companions include lady's slippers (all species), rose pogonia, grass pinks, and white and orange fringed orchids. Other interesting members of the same habitats include the carnivorous pitcher plant and sundews, bladderworts, and such heath-family representatives as rhodora, Labrador tea, and cranberry.

Arethusa ranges from Newfoundland to Minnesota and Ontario southward through the Great Lakes states to New Jersey, then very intermittently and locally southward to North Carolina in the mountains. Too difficult to be cultivated by any ordinary means, this wild orchid should be appreciated in the wilderness beauty of its bogland home.

SLIDE 36 ❧ **Northern Pitcher Plant, Huntsman's-Horn**
Sarracenia purpurea L.

Carnivorous plants always excite people. At first it is the idea that a plant can trap and consume an insect. But as enthusiasts examine the plant itself, they become fascinated with the remarkable structures which have evolved so that the plant may capture prey. So it is with the pitcher plants. Three different families of pitcher plants occur, each having developed similar special devices.

The American pitcher plants belong to one family and occur chiefly in the South, with the eight to ten species found mainly in coastal-plain bogs from the Carolinas to Mississippi. One species has made its way northward into New Jersey's sandy pine-barren bogs and then jumped from there northward into the abundant sphagnum peat bogs created by glacial events of the Ice Age. Following these bogs northward, the northern pitcher plant has become widespread across the Northeastern states and eastern Canada. The westward limits of the species in glaciated Canada are uncertain, but reports from Great Bear Lake and the discovery of a bog full of the plants along the Alaska Highway indicate a much more extensive Canadian range than had been supposed.

The leaf of the pitcher plant forms a hollow cup or pitcher that is semidecumbent and supported by mosses, grasses, or other pitchers. There is a spoutlike hood on one side of the leaf apex and a tightly rolled rim on the other. Along the side toward the plant stem and rhizome is a broad wing. The veins of the leaf and often the entire leaf tissue are colored in various shades of deep red maroon.

Around the rim of the pitcher, and along the margins of the spoutlike hood, there are glands which secrete fluids attractive to visiting insects. The fluids probably contain narcotic or muscle-relaxant substances. Insects feeding on the juices wander carelessly into the pitcher orifice. On the inside of the hood numerous down-pointing hairs make descent into the pitcher easy but egress difficult. Across the orifice from the hood the smooth, slippery, rolled rim makes it almost impossible for the insect to grip the edge.

In our species, the interior of the pitcher normally is about half filled with rainwater. Once an insect falls into the pitcher and becomes immersed, it rarely negotiates the slippery sides of the pitcher. Even if it does escape, numerous observations confirm that once trapped, insects seem confused and frequently wander back into the trap again. Eventually the pitcher plant wins many if not most battles; the insect drowns and sinks to the bottom of the trap, and digestive enzymes from the leaf decompose its body. The leaf absorbs various nutrients, especially nitrogen compounds. These essential compounds are usually deficient in bog soils, hence these remarkable adaptations.

In June, the pitcher plant sends up a flowering scape to a height of 3 to 5 dm. Atop the reflexed scape is a single, large, nodding globose flower 3 to 6 cm broad and of remarkable structure. Five leathery, glossy, maroon and green sepals form the outer flower envelope. Inside these and alternating with them are five pendant, spatulate, distally expanded maroon petals. Innermost in the flower is a globose ovary, its style remarkably expanded into a large five-pointed umbrella. Below each umbrella point lies a tiny, nipplelike, pollen-receptive stigma. The petals are so arranged in the flower as to function like one-way swinging doors. If a visiting bee pushes against the petal itself, it merely jams shut against the sides of the style umbrella, denying entrance to the insect. But if the insect enters over the style tips and stigma, between the petals, it can walk right in over the receptive stigma. Any pitcher-plant pollen the visitor may be carrying therefore falls on the stigma and effects cross-pollination. When leaving the flower, the insect can emerge anywhere, for pressure applied to the petals now swings them out and away from the stigma. The entire remarkable blossom structure, while not preventing self-pollination completely, works to encourage cross-pollination.

In spite of the insect-catching abilities of pitcher plants, several species of insects have adapted to life in or on pitcher plants. Larvae of several moth species feed on leaf or seedpod tissue. Most remarkable is the mosquito *Wyomia*, which lays its eggs exclusively within the rain-filled insect traps. Special hovering adaptations in the adults and a mucus envelope which prevents digestion of the larvae protect the insects. The mosquito larvae feed upon the carcasses of trapped insects.

The pitcher plant is one of our most unusual, showy, and interesting wild flowers. It can be cultivated in a bog garden or naturalized in acid bog soils or wet sands. In spite of its Northern distribution, the rhizome does not tolerate hard freezing. If it is grown outside in pots or tubs, precautions must be taken to keep the rhizome from freezing during the winter. In cultivation, pitcher plant demands nearly full sunlight for normal leaf development.

It is unfortunate that the current popularity of insectivorous plants has resulted in mass collections of pitcher plants, especially in the South. These are now sold in garden stores to the unaware who fail to perceive the need for acid soil or proper growing conditions. Hence, most of the plants perish.

SLIDE 37 ✿ **Grass Pink, Calopogon**
Calopogon pulchellus (Salisb.) R. Br.
(now generally referred to as *C. tuberosus*)

This delightful orchid still abounds in many an open bog glade or peaty meadow. Its very showy blooms appear in late June but occasional plants may be found in bloom as late as early August.

From a firm, fleshy, acorn-sized corm springs usually a single, strongly ribbed, almost plicate, grasslike leaf. The leaf is responsible for the name "grass" in grass pink, while the delicate magenta to pink bloom supplies the remainder of the name. The flower scape produces from three to as many as fifteen or more buds and blossoms. Essentially, the flowers open in upward succession on the scape, but it is not unusual to find several open and in good condition at once. Each flower is 2.5 to 4.5 cm broad, sessile, and borne on a somewhat zigzag rachis. The floral segments are slightly concave, with sepals and petals much alike. The most distinctive feature of the flower is the lip, which is carried uppermost in the flower. This is the morphologically normal position for an orchid's lip, but in most other species the lip is positioned as the lowermost floral segment by a twist in the ovary-pedicel below the bloom. The hinged lip, which is wedge-shaped and somewhat truncated at the tip, bears numerous fleshy processes tipped yellow and crimson. This beardlike feature has been recently interpreted by some biologists as a lure representing false pollen masses. According to this view, the bumblebees and other pollinators are attracted to the flower by the sight of the false pollen and alight directly upon the supposed pollen feast. The heavy bee is immediately and forcefully dropped against the flower stigma by its own weight and the hinged base of the lip. While struggling, the bee, if bearing calopogon pollen, effects cross-pollination.

A wide-ranging plant, grass pink occurs from Newfoundland to Minnesota, southwestward through the Great Lakes states, and southward locally in the Blue Ridge Mountains and even in Arkansas, but most abundantly in sandy coastal-plain bogs to Florida, Texas, and into Cuba and the Bahama Islands.

Primarily a peat-bog plant in our area, the species also grows in damp meadows, moist prairies, lake shores, and even roadside ditches. In the northern Great Lakes regions, calopogon frequently invades artificial boggy habitats such as borrow pits and the damp floors of abandoned gravel pits. It prefers acid soil, but it occurs in limey or marly bogs, usually growing on mossy tufts elevated above the alkaline waters.

Like most orchids, grass pinks are protected plants today. Yet they are not nearly so rare as many orchids with which they may share the same habitat. One reason is that the plants spread and develop not only by seed —a long, slow process in terrestrial orchids— but also by small offsets from the root.

Although the species may be cultivated, it is not easy to grow. Planting in a specially prepared soil of silica sand and peat offers the best garden result. The plants may be naturalized in naturally boggy, acid ground by planting tubers or scattering the dustlike seed. As the small corms, rich in vanillin, are much favored by meadow mice, means must be taken to protect them in the wild garden.

SLIDE 38 ❁ **Rose Pogonia, Snakemouth**
Pogonia ophioglossoides (L.) Ker.

Where arethusa blooms in early June, in July you usually will find the dainty rose pogonia. Although local, this is not really a rare orchid in its range except where human activity has destroyed its habitat. The plant demands very wet soils, reveling in deep saturated beds of sphagnum moss, often right at the margin of a pond or boggy lake, or in the wet sand of a pine-barren or coastal-plain swamp. Only rarely does it venture into drier peaty meadows. Once I found it in damp crevices in granite cliffs in the Carolina Blue Ridge Mountains.

Rose pogonia grows from East Texas to Long Island in sandy coastal bogs or Cumberland Plateau swamps. It extends northward to Newfoundland, westward to Minnesota, and southward to Illinois, Indiana, and Pennsylvania, growing chiefly in sphagnum bogs.

The plant spreads from root runners as well as from seed. Often whole colonies proliferate vegetatively and fail to bloom for several years. But the single, fleshy, oblong-lanceolate leaves can be found in masses. When the plant does bloom, the erect stem reaches a height of 0.5 to 6 dm and bears a single, obovate, fleshy green leaf near its middle. The shape, size, texture, and carriage of the leaf and the flower bud of the pogonia strongly resemble the aspect of the adder's-tongue fern, *Ophioglossum;* hence the Latin name of the orchid. The blossom is 1 to 3 cm long, with the sepals and petals much alike, rose pink to white in color and darker along the veins. The lip is larger, widest at its apex, and bears rows of numerous erect, fleshy tubercles or processes.

Henry David Thoreau described the odor of the flower as like that of garter snakes, a most unappetizing comparison and one I have not found so. I interpret the odor as fruitlike, resembling red raspberries, and quite pleasing. In calm weather it is strong enough so that one can often detect the presence of the orchid before actually seeing it in the lush bog vegetation.

Although now widely protected, the plant seems to be in no real danger except from habitat destruction. It is not easily cultivated in the wild garden, but it may be quite easily grown in the cool greenhouse in live sphagnum in a plastic pot kept moist with distilled water. It also grows well in a mixture of silica sand and peat. Rose pogonia is one of the few orchids which can generate plantlets at its root tips and along the creeping rootstalk. Well-grown pot plants reward the grower with much vegetative reproduction, often crowding the pot.

SLIDE 39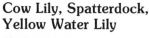

Cow Lily, Spatterdock, Yellow Water Lily
Nuphar spp.

In North America, cow lilies form a characteristic part of the wetlands vegetation, growing in ponds, eutrophying lakes, troughs, and sloughs in bogs. Sometimes the plants, poking their leaves and flowers up through beds of loose peat, mosses, and accumulated plant debris, give evidence of how recently the spot had been open water before the events of plant succession covered it.

Germinating on the mucky or peaty bottom beneath shallow waters, cow lilies develop at first only subsurface aquatic leaves. In at least one Southern species, these seedlings are collected and sold to aquarium fanciers as the underwater "banana" plant. As plants mature, large, firm, and tough lily pads float or stand above the water's surface, depending upon the nature of the species. The creeping rhizomes of the plant are enormous, often as thick in diameter as a fencepost, and are pocked with old leaf scars. A single large plant may cover many square feet of lake bed in one season, producing hundreds of pounds of organic matter. Much of this rootstock decays slowly behind growing tips; the plant therefore makes a major contribution to the filling of lakes and ponds.

The cuplike, 6- to 10-cm-broad yellow flowers usually stand above the surface of the water rather than float, as do those of the white water lilies. It is the sepals, yellow in all species, and not the petals, which form the colorful part of the bloom. The true petals are small, inconspicuous, and inserted with the numerous stamens. The large central ovary bears a disk with nine to twenty stigmatic rays.

The edible seeds of spatterdocks, when removed from their rather firm shells, were much used by Indians of the Pacific Northwest. East of the Rockies the Indians utilized the rootstocks, mainly as a starchy vegetable.

The plant is easily cultivated and worthy of greater use in the garden. It grows well in ponds and tubs, or becomes naturalized in shallow waters. Most of the species are not rare. It is characteristic of the flowers of these water lilies often to be heavily infested by unsightly black aphids during the heat of summer.

SLIDE 40 ❦ **White Fringed Orchid**

Habenaria blephariglottis (Willd.) Hook.

Two groups of fringed orchids occur in Eastern North America, one with the lip of the flower divided into three wedge-shaped fringed sections and the other with the lip a solid tongue-shaped organ with fringed margins. In both groups we find some spectacularly beautiful orchids.

The white fringed orchid is a member of the tongue-shaped-lip group. It grows over a very extensive area, perhaps with a greater range of latitude than any other fringed species. Frequent in pine-barren sandy bogs in New Jersey, it occurs northward in peaty sphagnum bogs and swamps of glacial regions to Newfoundland, and west to lower Michigan. In the South, it is found most frequently in wet pine-barren bogs or clearings in damp sandy soil. It is also common on the coastal plain and in a few bogs on the Cumberland Plateau. Although totally absent in many districts, it is locally abundant in others.

In the North, it is commonest in well-lighted open glades among groves of tamarack and black spruce in deep-piled sphagnum. Here it shares habitats with pitcher plants, sundews, cranberry, moccasin flowers, rose pogonias, bog false solomon's seal, bog rosemary, and bog laurel. It blooms in late July and early August.

The 1- to 1.5-cm-long flowers grow in a racemelike spike of from eight to forty or more blossoms. Most forms display a sparkling, snowy white lip, although the backs of petals and sepals may show some green or cream tones. Each 1-cm-long tonguelike lip has long eyelashlike projections on the margins, and the back of the lip is produced backward and downward into a long, curved, hollow spur which bears a drop of nectar near its base. To obtain the nectar, a visiting moth or insect must so position itself in the bloom as to effect cross-pollination if it is carrying pollen.

White fringed orchids vary in height with habitats, exposure, and race of the plant, and range from to 1 to 6 dm tall. The two or three strongly keeled and pointed blue-green leaves partially sheath the stem. Upper leaves become reduced to leafy bracts subtending each bloom. Beneath the peaty soil the plant produces yearly a completely new set of long, fleshy, tuberoid roots covered with tiny white root hairs. Plants usually occur singly but occasionally form clumps. The most spectacular clumps I have seen grew in a bog where local residents picked highbush blueberries. The crushing of the plants underfoot by berry pickers in late summer seemed to stimulate clump formation. In years when the blueberries failed and the swamps were unmolested, the densely packed flowering colonies looked almost like lingering snowbanks among the tall blueberry bushes.